John Paul Rylands

An attempt to identify the arms formerly existing in the

windows of the parish church and Austin Friary at

Warrington

John Paul Rylands

**An attempt to identify the arms formerly existing in the windows of the parish church and Austin Friary at Warrington**

ISBN/EAN: 9783337261207

Printed in Europe, USA, Canada, Australia, Japan

Cover: Foto ©Lupo / pixelio.de

More available books at **www.hansebooks.com**

# Arms formerly in Warrington Church.

**Dutton.**

**Boteler, Baron of Warrington.**

**Gerard, of Bryn.**

**Dutton, Troutbeck, & Boteler.**

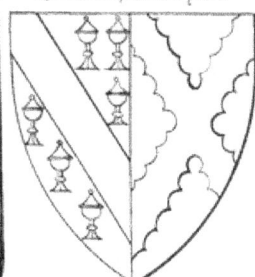

**Boteler impaling Delves.**

**Boteler & Clyderhou?**

**Rixton of Rixton.**

**Masey of Rixton.**

**Standish. ancient.**

i. Rixton. ii. Masey.
iii. Penington. iv. Sorton.

**Troutbeck.—ancient.**

# AN ATTEMPT

TO IDENTIFY

# THE ARMS

FORMERLY EXISTING IN THE WINDOWS

OF THE

# PARISH CHURCH

AND

# AUSTIN FRIARY

AT

# WARRINGTON.

BY

WILLIAM BEAMONT, ESQ.

AND

J. PAUL RYLANDS, F.S.A.

WARRINGTON:
PERCIVAL PEARSE, 8, SANKEY STREET.
1878.

# PREFACE.

" Such is the despight, not so much of time as of malevolent people, to all antiquities,
especially of this kind, that it may be well to place on record what we know of these family
memorials."— *Weever's Funeral Monuments.*

THE memorials which a past age has left us, apt as they are at
times to be overlooked, are still worthy of remembrance, for,
by linking the present with the past and awakening the imagination,
they break the dull routine of every-day business, and, by thus giving
us, as it were, a new sense, they seem to make life both longer and
more pleasant.

The painting and staining of glass for windows, an art which has
some connexion with the following pages, though not ascending to
classic times, may still lay claim to a respectable antiquity, since the
decorated windows of the Abbey Church of Tegernsee, in Upper
Bavaria, which were executed as early as the latter half of the tenth
century, shew that the art had already passed beyond the period of in-
fancy; while, if the tradition be true which is existing in one of our good
English families, that Charlemagne, from whom they claim ancestry,
was its patron, and was also the first to introduce painted windows
into churches, the art had not only an illustrious patron, but its
origin is carried back to the very beginning of the ninth century.    In
the early stages of the art a painted window was only produced by
making a pattern in outline with finely-made leaden frames, into the
grooves of which pieces of stained glass were then inserted and fitted.
In this respect, however, the revival of the art in modern times, when
pictures exhibiting the painter's art on sheets of glass of almost any
size can be produced with little or none of the original clumsy framing,
must be considered to have made a great advance upon the art in its
first original.

*b*

In England we are told that stained glass in connexion with architecture was first used in the thirteenth century, during the reign of our Henry III.,[*] and this statement of our English historians is confirmed by a high French authority,[†] who adds that in the same century the art came into very extensive use in England. The art, in consequence of the great attention paid to it, improved rapidly from its first introduction into England, and it soon became the handmaid of the herald's gentle science, which attained its zenith in the time of Richard II., when every gentleman bore coat armour and resented any infringement of it as a great wrong, as may be seen from the Scrope and Grosvenor controversy, in which there were not less than 184 witnesses examined, amongst whom, besides one or more princes, were Owen Glendower and the poet Chaucer, and in which the parties must have spent a fortune. Richard II. expended a large sum in filling one of the great windows of Canterbury Cathedral with his arms and cognisances, and Edward IV., calling to mind what his last predecessor of the house of York had done, followed his example by a munificent present of painted glass to fill another of the great windows of the same cathedral, and most of our cathedrals and many of our parish churches soon glowed with the rich colours thrown on their walls and pavements from their richly-decorated windows. In the reign of the former monarch, or before, in consequence of its almost universal use, stained glass had made another march in the path of improvement. Public taste had advanced, and artists, having grown more ambitious, instead of paying exclusive attention to heraldic designs, sought to illuminate the greater windows of our cathedrals and churches with subjects from Scripture or of historic interest.

The windows at Canterbury told in detail the story of the life and death of Becket, their celebrated prelate, in a language which appealed to the eye, and which the most illiterate could read and understand. But Canterbury was not alone, for many another cathedral and church

---

[*] Dallaway's *Anecdotes of the Arts in England*, 1830, and the same author's *Architecture in England*, 1833.

[†] De Caumont's *French Archæology*.

could boast of a similar display of decorated windows, with designs in a high style of art, some of which equalled those of Fairford Church, which have fortunately been preserved, and on which volumes of criticism have deservedly been written. Many of these windows commemorated the actions of saints who were but little known, and Shakspere, whom nothing escaped, and who had probably seen what he has noticed in some church window, makes "Borachio" the follower of Don John, tell "Conrade" that the young men of the time in their devotion to fashion sometimes aped "the God Bel's priests in the old church window."* The poet in his allusion meant to rally the young boasters of his day who appeared in slashed garments as if they had been wounded, in which evil case Baal's priests really appeared after Elijah had taunted them on Carmel.

But we have another poet's evidence that the beautiful ornament — a painted window — was not exclusively confined to a church, but was met with also in the houses of the great, as witness the following passage :

> And sothe to saine my chamber was
> Full well depainted and with glas
> Were all the windows, wel yglased
> Full clere and not a hole ycrased,
> That to behold it was great joy
> For wholly all the storie of Troy
> Was in the glassing ywrought thus.
>
> *(Chaucer's Dreame,* fo. 241*.)*

The palmy periods of decorated glass for windows were the 13th, the 15th, and the 17th centuries. In the first of those periods it was full of youthful vigour, the second was its age of manhood, and the third was its period of revival, when under Charles I., a monarch who loved art, painters of some name were attracted to designing and executing church windows.

If we inquire what were the motives which led our ancestors to fill their church windows with these beautiful architectural decorations we shall find them to be principally the following :

* *Much Ado about Nothing,* iii, 3.

I. In a dark age to erect a painted window that should induce or deepen devotion was esteemed a work of merit which would conciliate the favour of heaven, and an old poet puts this argument into the mouth of a friar in addressing a rich female penitent :

> He assoyled her soon, and sithen he said
> We have a window in working will set us full high,
> Woldest the glase the window, and therein thy name grave
> Seker should thy soul be heaven to have.
>
> *(Piers Plowman,* fo. 12.)

II. A history told in pictures either on the walls or in the windows of a church could be understood even by the unlearned. The whole history of the Old Testament is thus told on the walls of the chapter house at Salisbury, and many a painted window has taught its lessons to the peasant who had no book learning.

III. Again, a painted window was often set up to the pious remembrance of some deceased relative or connexion — a husband, a wife, or other dear relation — and addressing the bystander, as of old, with a " siste viator," it often besought him to offer up a prayer for the deceased, whose name and date of death it recorded, while it very often gave also his name who erected it.

IV. Sometimes the donor of a window was one who loved art, and, besides honouring God's house, had an æsthetic object in making his gift, thinking justly that

> Storied windows richly dight,
> Casting a dim religious light

gave solemnity to a sacred edifice, and were helps to devotion.

V. More frequently, however, a beautiful window was meant to perpetuate the memory of the donor's family, and to display before the reader's eye an heraldic page to aid the genealogist in tracing the family pedigree. Sometimes the same window contained the record of many generations of the same family, when to compare small things with great it resembled the " imagines avorum" of the old Romans.

But art, although proverbially long, enjoys no immunity either from violent changes, the caprices of taste, or those great outbreaks of religious or political zeal from which no institution is at all times safe. And "time which antiquates antiquities" had spared these glassy memorials for nearly six centuries, a longer date than has been vouchsafed to some less fragile and more substantial monuments, when that great event, the Reformation of Religion, brought about as much by the discovery of printing and the light of the printed books which it had sent abroad, as by the decision of king Henry VIII., occasioned a revolution in religious feeling which led to many of these painted windows being looked upon as superstitious, and awakened a zeal for their removal. This zeal, which produced its partial fruits in the reign of the monarch just mentioned, carried men still further in the next reign, and led to many of these windows being destroyed, more particularly those in which were pourtrayed the stories of saints which had begun to be discredited and thought superstitious. When an old antiquary could utter this feeling lamentation over antiquities—"Alas! our own noble monuments and precious antiquities which are the great beauty of our lande are as little regarded as the payringes of our nayles,"* his regret was general, and extended to antiquities in general, and had no special reference to the injury which church windows sustained through this zeal for religion, when the same cause which erected them — " sweet love changing its property " — led to their destruction. He had not the gift of prophecy, and did not foresee such scenes as occurred in France in the revolution of 1793, when the people broke into the churches and tore down the images of the saints and destroyed them by wholesale, exclaiming as they did it, " Ah! messieurs, you have ruled over us too long, but you shall do it no longer." But the attack on church windows sometimes fell upon such as had only armorial bearings, and had neither the story of saints nor other superstitious subjects in them. It had been well on such occasions if the assailants had been led by a leader as wise and as ready as he who, when the mob had broken into the Cathedral of Chartres to destroy a beautiful group of statues, diverted them from their purpose and saved the statues by placing his red cap on the head of the principal figure and transforming

* Weever's *Funeral Monuments.*

it from a figure of the Virgin into a statue of the Goddess of Reason.

In the first year of Queen Elizabeth's reign, by an act of Parliament for establishing religion, commissioners were appointed to visit every diocese to put it in force, by regulating church rites, ornaments and ceremonies, and, by another act of the same year, for suppressing all such religious houses as had been re-erected and set up by the late queen, the same commissioners were to see that all rood lofts and other images which had been set up in the churches were taken down and destroyed. This latter act, having received a somewhat wider interpretation than was intended, and some things not meant having been destroyed, an ordinance was issued restraining further demolition within certain limits, and its effect was to save much of the glass now remaining in our churches. Time and royal authority before the time of Charles I., having somewhat stayed the crusade against painted glass, and the king himself having a fine taste, had commissioned artists of merit to execute some painted windows for him, which led to a sort of revival of the art in an improved form, and without the superstitions objected to. But afterwards, when the great war between the king and the parliament broke out, the old destructive zeal revived, and there arose a cry,

> We'll break the windows which the Witch
> Of Babylon hath painted!

and, amongst others, a zealot at Canterbury, one Richard Culmer, commonly called Blue Dick, earned an unenviable renown by destroying the windows of that magnificent cathedral[*].

The decorated windows which adorned the parish church and the priory of the hermit friars of the Order of Saint Augustine at Warrington, of which an account is given in the following pages, were of various ages, from the 13th century down to the year 1527, now more than 350 years ago, when the latest window — that to the rector Delves — was set up. The decorations, except the figures of Thomas earl of Lancaster and his two knights Banastre and Holland, in which

---

[*] Britton's *Cathedral Antiquities*, vol, i, pp. 71-2.

there was nothing superstitious, consisted exclusively of shields of
arms, and to this cause, probably, it is owing that they were existing
unimpaired in 1572 and 1640, when the two separate accounts of them
were taken.   How they fared a few years after the latter year, when
the civil troubles were at their height, we do not know; but, except
the shield of rector Delves, which remained unimpaired until 1860,
when the church was restored — and even this solitary shield perished
— none of them existed until the first year of the present century.   Of
the thirty-five families whom the shields commemorated, the Leghs, the
Leighs, the Warburtons and the Gerards alone remain connected with
the neighbourhood ; of all the rest, their names as territorial owners
have disappeared and their places now know them no more.   Such is
the mighty change which time has made, and that which the oldest
poet said is as true now as when he wrote it :

> Like leaves on trees the race of man is found,
> Now green in youth, now withering on the ground ;
> Another race the following spring supplies,
> They fall successive and successive rise.
> So generations in their course decay,
> So flourish these when those have past away.
>
> *(Pope's Homer*, B, vi.)

# PART I.

## 𝕿𝖍𝖊 𝕬𝖗𝖒𝖘 𝖜𝖍𝖎𝖈𝖍 𝖋𝖔𝖗𝖒𝖊𝖗𝖑𝖞 𝖊𝖝𝖎𝖘𝖙𝖊𝖉 𝖎𝖓 𝖙𝖍𝖊 𝕎𝖎𝖓𝖉𝖔𝖜𝖘 𝖆𝖓𝖉 𝖔𝖓 𝖙𝖍𝖊 𝕸𝖔𝖓𝖚𝖒𝖊𝖓𝖙𝖘 𝖎𝖓 𝕎𝖆𝖗𝖗𝖎𝖓𝖌𝖙𝖔𝖓 𝕮𝖍𝖚𝖗𝖈𝖍, 𝖜𝖎𝖙𝖍 𝖆𝖓 𝖆𝖙𝖙𝖊𝖒𝖕𝖙 𝖙𝖔 𝖆𝖘𝖘𝖎𝖌𝖓 𝖙𝖍𝖊𝖒 𝖙𝖔 𝖙𝖍𝖊𝖎𝖗 𝖕𝖗𝖔𝖕𝖊𝖗 𝖔𝖜𝖓𝖊𝖗𝖘.

A MONG the *Harleian Manuscripts*, preserved in the British Museum, there are two sets of notes, made nearly seventy years apart, of the coats of arms and ornaments which formerly adorned the windows and monuments in Warrington Church. The first notes are supposed to have been taken by Sampson Erdeswicke, the Historian of Staffordshire, in the year 1572; the second were taken by Randle Holme of Chester, in the year 1640.

These memoranda consist of abbreviated descriptions, with, in some few cases, very rude drawings. In the following copies of the notes it has been thought desirable to extend the abbreviations; and also, for convenience of reference, to make occasional additions, which will be found placed in square brackets.

When Randle Holme took his notes he described many shields that occur in Erdeswicke's memoranda; those arms which are noted both by Erdeswicke and Holme are therefore marked by asterisks to prevent confusion, and to point out such as had been erected after 1572.

## EXTENDED BLAZON OF SAMPSON ERDESWICKE'S NOTES OF ARMS IN WARRINGTON CHURCH, TAKEN 1572.
### (*Harleian MSS.*, 2129, art. 164, fol. 73.)

### AT WARRINGTON CHURCH.

[1.] Azure, a bend between six [covered] cups Or, quartered with Argent, a lion rampant Gules, for *Boteler de Beasea* [*Bewsey*].

[2.] *Boteler* [as above but without the quartering] impaled with *Delves* [*of Dodington*, co. Chester] viz : Argent a chevron Gules, fretty Or, between three delves or turves Sable.

[3.] Argent, three bendlets [enhanced] Gules, on the Tomb. [*Byron.*]

*[4.] Azure, a lion rampant Ermine [crowned Or]. [*Gerard of Bryn.*] and

D

*[5.] Argent, a cross, and in the first quarter a fleur de lys Sable. [*Haydock of Haydock.*] and

*[6.] *Duttons*, Quarterly Argent and Gules, in the second and third a fret Or.

*[7.] Argent, a cross Gules. [*St. George.*]

*[8.] Gules, a cross [engrailed] Argent. [*Legh.*]

[9.] Argent, three barrulets [? bendlets enhanced] Gules. [? *Byron.*]

[10.] Argent, a chevron between three storks [? cormorants] Sable. [? *Warburton of Arley.*]

*[11.] Sable, a chevron between three crosses patente [? patonce] Argent, a crescent of the first for difference. [*Southworth.*]

[12.] Another [the same shield] with an Annulet Sable for difference. [*Southworth.*]

*[13.] *Dutton.* [As No. 6.]

*[14.] Argent, a lion rampant Gules.

*[15.] Azure, a bend between six [covered] cups Or. [*Boteler.*]

*[16.] Argent, a chevron between three pierced mullets Sable. [*Bruche of Bruche.*]

*[17.] Argent, on a bend Sable, three [covered] cups of the field. [*Rixton of Rixton.*]

*[18.] Azure, five fusils in fesse Or, each charged with a torteau. [*Plumpton.*]

*[19.] *Botelier* quarterlie againe. [As No. 1.]

*[20.] *Boteler* impaled with *Delves.* [As No. 2.] and

*[21.] *Delves* alone [Argent, a chevron Gules fretty Or, between three delves or turves Sable.]

* Ther lieth buried one Ric[hard] Delves, Canon of Leichfeld and parson of Warrington obiit 23 Novembr 1527.

[22.] Argent on a bend Sable, three lozenges Argent [each charged with a saltire Gules.] [? *Urswick.*]

*[23.] Another *Boteler.* [As No. 15.]

[24.] Another *Boteler.* [As No. 15.]

*[25.] Argent, a lion rampant Gules.

*[26.] Quarterly of four, 1st, Argent on a bend Sable, three cups Argent [of the field] [*Rixton of Rixton*], 2nd, quarterly Gules and Argent, in the second a mullet Sable. [*Mascy of Rixton.*] 3rd, Argent a fesse Vert between three parrots Gules. [*Pennington.*] 4th, Argent a squirrel sejant Gules. [*Horton of Horton.*] *Massye of Rixton* in Nova Capella. [Referring to No. 26.]

[27.] [A drawing of the following.] Quarterly, 1st and 4th, grand quarters, Argent, on a bend Sable, three fishes Or. [*Sankey of Sankey*] 2nd and 3rd, grand quarters, quarterly. 1st and 4th Argent, three chevronels between as many birds Gules. [? *Singleton.*] 2nd, Sable [? Vert] a camel passant Argent [? *Fallowes.*] 3rd, Azure, a chevron between three garbs Or. [? *Hatton.*]

[28.] Gules, a saltier engrailed Or [? *Clyderhou*] upon the garments of Boteler's wife and Boteler himself, therewith as a coat of arms; Argent, on a saltier Sable a pierced mullet Or, within a bordure engrailed Sable [of the second.] [? *Standish, ancient.*]

[In] le Nova Capella *illis*:

[29.] Quarterly, 1st and 4th, Argent, on a bend Sable three cups covered Argent. [*Rixton of Rixton.*] 2nd, Quarterly, Gules and Argent, in the second a mullet Sable. [*Mascy of Rixton.*] 3rd, Argent, a fesse Vert between three parrots Gules. [*Pennington.*]

[30.] Quarterly, 1st and 4th, Argent, on a bend Sable three fishes Or. [*Sankey of Sankey.*] 2nd and 3rd, Sable, three fusils palewise Argent.

In an owld wyndowe:

[31.] Quarterly, Argent and Gules, in the first a mullet Sable. [*Mascy of Rixton.*]

---

## NOTES OF WARRINGTON CHURCH, TAKEN BY ME, RANDLE HOLME, 1640.
### (*Harleian MSS.*, 2129, art. 269, fo. 184.)

In the Chappell on the South side against Butler's Chappell is an Auntient Monument of a man in armore lyinge under an arch in the wall and reported to be a *Massy*; it is called Massy's Chapel.

In the Quier on the South side in the window a man in armor kneelinge, on his brest & shoulders *Buttler's* cote, and his wife kneelinge against him, on her surcote is Butler's cote, also in the window above is Butler's cote.

In windows on same side:

*[32.] Argent, a lion rampant Gules.

[33.] Gules, a saltier engrailed Or, in severall escutions. [? *Clyderhou.*]

*[34.] In the Est window in the Chancell [there is] only *Butler's* cote very Auntient. [As in No. 15.]

In the highest window on the South side.

*[35.] Argent, a chevron between three pierced mullets Sable. [*Bruche of Bruche.*]

*[36.] Argent, a chevron between three crosses patonce Sable, a crescent of the first for difference. *Southworth.*

In the highest window on the North side :

⁰ [37.] Gules, a cross engrailed Argent. *Legh*

⁰[38.] Argent, a cross Gules. *St. Geo[rge.]*

In the next window on [the] same side :—

ᵇ[39.] Argent, a cross Sable, in the first quarter a fleur de lys Sa. [of the second.] *Hadod [i.e. Haydock of Haydock.]*

ᵈ[40.] Azure, a lion rampant Ermine, crowned Or. *Gerord. [i.e. Gerard of Bryn.]*

*[41.] Quarterly, Argent and Gules, in the second and third a fret Or. *Dutton.*

*[41a] In the Chancell is a faire marble stone inlayd wᵗʰ brass & pillars and turretts, and in brasse is therin a man wᵗʰ a curious cote Embrauthered [embroidered] prayinge, and standinge at his feete *Delves'* cote and writ under : OF YOUR CHARITY PRAY FOR THE SOULE OF MR. RICHARD DELVES, CANON IN THE CATHEDRALL CHURCH OF LICHFEILD AND PARSON OF THIS CHURCH OF WARINGTON, DYED THE xxii OF NOVEMBER THE YEARE OF OUR LORD GOD MDXXVII.

In an Escution in the Chancell *Hawardyn [of Woolston]* cote viz :

[42] Quarterly, 1st, Argent, guttée [de poix] and a fesse nebulée Sable. [*Hawarden.*] 2nd, Argent, a bend fusilly Sable [*Legh of High Legh ancient*]. 3rd, Gules, a pale fusilly Argent, [*Lymme of Lymm*]. 4th, Quarterly 1st and 4th, Argent a wolf passant Sable. *Woolston [of Woolston]*; 2nd and 3rd, quarterly Argent and Sable, a cross patonce counterchanged. *Hawarden [Eaton.]*

In Butler's Chapel on the North side is a very Auntient monum[en]t of a man in Armore cutt in Stone in an arch of the wall.

In the midde [middle] of the Chapell is a faire tombe of Butler with his wife lyinge as the Toumb of Troutbeck in St. Marye's in Chester with shields all about, but all the cotes be worne off.

In the windowes there :

*[43.] *Dutton's* cote. [As No. 6.]

*[44.] Argent, a lion rampant Gules. *Legh [? of High Legh.]*

*[45.] *Butler's* cote. [As No. 15.]

*[46.] Azure, five fusils [in fesse] Or, each charged with a torteau. [*Plumpton.*]

In the Est [East] window is written ORATE P' ANIMA THO BUTLER, MILITI. ᵉᵗ PSPO [sic for pro prospero] STATU DNE. MARGRETE BUTLER VIDUE AC THO. BUTLER AR. AC OĪBUS FILIARŪ. D'CTE MARGARETE QUE MARGARETA HANC FENESTRAM FIERI FECIT ANᴼ. DNI. M.CCCC.XXIIII. [Pray for the soul of Sir Thomas Butler, knight, and for the good estate of Dame Margaret Butler, widow, and Thomas Butler, esquire, and all the daughters of the said Margaret; which Margaret had this window made in the year of our Lord 1524.]

In the same window is *[47] *Butler* and [48] *Redish* cotes quarterly [exactly as No. 1], and two figures, he kneelinge in armor and a sonne after [*i.e.* behind] him, and she with 7 daughters after [behind] her.

*[49.] There is Butler and Delves Impaled [as No. 20], and also *[49*a*] *Delves'* cote alone [as No. 21.]

In the said chapell on a fine marble stone at the west end of the Tombe in brasse is two figures, a man standing in armore w[th] *Butler's* cote on : and on his wives' cote is *Delves'* cote. The 4 Evangelests in brass in the 4 corners, and written about [around] : PRAY FOR THE SOULES OF THO: BUTLER, KT. AND DAME MARGRET HIS WIFE W[CH] HAD ONE SONNE AND 8 DAUGHTERS. VILZT : THOMAS, MAR-RIED CICELY DAU: TO PIERS LEIGH, MARGRET TO RICH: BOULD, KT., ELLEN TO JO: BAGOTT, [ELIZABETH] TO GEO: BOOTH, ISABELL TO RANDLE BRERETON, ANNE TO GEO: ATHERTON, CICELY TO HENRY KVGHLEY, MARGERY TO THO: SOUTHWORTH, AND DOROTHY, SR. THOMAS DYED THE 27 APRELL 1522.

No more Monuments or Armes in the Church.

---

In *Harleian MSS.*, 2129, art. 270, fol. 185, are the following notes :

In Buttler's Chappell in Warrington Church,

[50.] *Buttler.* [As before.]

[51.] Argent, a lion rampant Gules.

[52.] Dutton. [As before.]

[53.] Azure, six [? five] fusils in fesse Or, each charged with an escallop shell Gules. [*Plumpton.*]

[54.] *Butler* [quartering Argent a lion rampant Gules.]

[55.] *Butler* and the lion rampant quarterly, impaling *Delves.*

Mergrett daughter to Delves ma[rried] Thoms. Buttler. ye lyke is rightten in a wyndowe. Dna. M'greta Buttler vid'. 1423 [? 1483] she kneleth in ye. wyn-dow her roabes garnished with the armes of Delves. Thome Buttler, ar. [esquire] her husband made that wyndow.

In the same chappell buryed one Buttler in allablaster with sundry armes about them, viz :

[56.] Dutton. [As No. 6.] [57.] *Troutbeck* [Argent, three moors' heads couped proper,] and *Buttler* [as before] quarterly. Then [58] *Troutbeck* single, viz : Argent, three moryeux heeds [moors' heads] Sable. Then [59] *Ratcliff* [? Argent, a bend engrailed Sable] impaled with *Byron* [as No. 3], and in the last squtchon [escutcheon]. [60.] *Massy of Rixton* [as No. 31.]

# Notes.

No. 1. The arms of the family of Boteler of Bewsey, *after c.* 1330, the quartering having come into the family on the marriage of Sir William Boteler and Elizabeth. This quartering occurs so frequently in the *MSS.*, either alone or as a quarter of the Botelers, that it evidently indicates an alliance of no ordinary importance; it is therefore the more to be regretted that up to the present time every attempt to ascertain to what family dame Elizabeth Boteler belonged has been without success. The same coat is impaled with the Boteler arms upon a seal, inscribed **S' ELIZAB' LE BOTELER**, which dame Elizabeth appended to a charter in the year 1346, and a cast of the seal may be seen in the Warrington museum. Many families bore a red lion rampant on a white shield, among others we may name Legh, Reddish, Hulton, Lostock, Astley, Turbeville, Brewse and Mountford. In the *MSS.* it is sometimes called Legh and sometimes Redish, but we have no proof that it belonged to either family.

Nos. 2, 20, 21, 49, 49*a*, and the monument described after 49*a*, commemorate Sir Thomas Boteler, and Margaret his wife, the daughter of Sir John Delves of Dodington, co. Chester, who was killed at the battle of Tewkesbury. The Delves coat of arms has a curious history: Sir John Delves, afterwards esquire of the body to king Edward III, was present at the battle of Poictiers, and as one of the four celebrated esquires of James, Lord Audley, knight of the garter, was in a very great measure instrumental in obtaining the victory. " After the battle, Edward the Black Prince retained Lord Audley in his service for life, and granted him 500 marks out of his revenue in England, which he bestowed on his four esquires, Delves, Hawkestone, Fouleshurst and Mackworth, whereupon the prince, having thanked him for so doing, gave him 600 marks per annum more, and in remuneration of these signal services, all the four esquires added part of Lord Audley's arms to their own." Lord Audley's arms were Gules, fretty Or, and the chevron of the Delves coat was changed from some other tincture on this occasion. The delves, or turves, were borne in allusion to the name, as representing turves of earth taken up separately by a spade.

The marriage of Sir Thomas Boteler and dame Margaret took place about the year 1480, and the shield, No. 55, where by mistake she is called Dña and Vid. and a wrong date is given, was put in soon after.

Richard Delves, rector of Warrington (Nos. 21 and 41*a*) and brother to dame Margaret, was the third son of Sir John Delves.

Nos. 3 and 9. The arms of the family of Byron, possibly placed there to commemorate Sir Nicholas Byron, who married Alice, the daughter of Sir John and dame Isabella Butler, in the reign of Henry VI.

Nos. 4 and 40. The ancient arms of the knightly family of Gerard of Bryn, which they abandoned in the sixteenth century for the arms of Fitzgerald (Argent, a saltier Gules) to denote the origin of their family; afterwards the lion rampant ermine was given as the crest.

This shield was probably put up about the time of Sir John Butler's marriage with the first of his three wives, Margaret, daughter of Peter Gerard of Bryn; this was in the year 1444. (*Lords of Warrington*, Chet. Soc., p. 263.)

Nos. 5 and 39. The arms of the ancient family of Haydock, of Haydock. The same coat is carved upon the tower of Winwick church in a separate shield, with the arms of Southworth in another, and casts of both shields are preserved in the Warrington museum. About the year 1403, Johanna, daughter and heiress of Sir Gilbert de Haydock, married Sir Peter Legh, of Lyme, Knight-banneret; after whose death she married Sir Richard Molyneux, and her interesting tomb may still be seen in Sefton church. The arms of Haydock were no doubt placed in Warrington church to commemorate Sir Gilbert de Haydock, great-grandfather of Johanna, who founded a chantry in Winwick church in 1330, and in 1348 purchased from Prior Richard Pygas a perpetual chantry in the house of the Carmelites at Chester. (*House of Lyme*, p. 26.) Sir Gilbert died about the year 1358, and it seems not unlikely that his arms were then placed in the church windows.

Nos. 6, 13, 41, 43, 52, and 56. The arms of the family of Dutton, which were sometimes used by their direct descendants, the Warburtons of Arley. Richard, eldest son of Sir William and dame Elizabeth Butler, married Johanna, daughter of Thomas Dutton; and Elizabeth, daughter of the same Sir William and dame Elizabeth, married Sir Piers Dutton about 1380.

Nos. 7 and 38. The red cross of St. George of England.

Nos. 8 and 37. The arms of several families of Legh. This cross engrailed, as it appears on some of the family seals, was originally a cross fusilly, the form in which it appears on the seal of the first Piers Legh of Lyme. Erdeswicke (No. 8) makes the cross plain, but there can be no doubt that this shield is identical with the one copied by Randle Holme (No. 37).

No. 10 had disappeared when Randle Holme took his notes. Erdeswicke calls the birds storks, but they were more likely cormorants, and were intended to commemorate some member of the family of Warburton of Arley.

Nos. 11 and 36, and No. 12. Nos. 11 and 36 describe the same pane of glass; No. 12 had disappeared in 1640. They represent two members of the Southworth family, a second and a fifth son, probably brothers. The Southworths, who took their name from the township of Southworth-with-Croft, in Winwick parish, became subsequently possessed, by marriage, of the estate of Samlesbury, near Preston, and were afterwards generally known as the Southworths of Samlesbury. The crosses in the arms are frequently drawn and described as cross-croslets, but there can be no doubt that they were originally crosses patonce; they are so depicted upon seals of the family used in 1347 and 1394, in a roll of arms *temp.* Richard II, and upon Winwick church tower. Margery, daughter of Sir Thomas Boteler, was married, about the year 1518, to Sir Thomas Southworth of Samlesbury, he having been divorced from his first wife Ann Stanley (*Lords of Warrington*, Chet. Soc., p. 415); but, as the arms in the window refer to a second and a fifth son, they cannot, either of them, be intended to commemorate Sir Thomas Southworth.

Nos. 16 and 35. The arms of the family of Bruche of Bruche. The same coat appears upon the seals of the family at various dates; but the seal of Gilbert del Bruche, in 1326, displays upon a shield, between the initials of his name, two lions passant-guardant in pale. The Bruches held Bruche from an early date until the reign of Queen Elizabeth, when Roger and Hamlet Bruche sold it to Sir Peter Legh of Lyme, whose son, Peter Legh of Bruche, esquire, was member of parliament for Newton, and dying 5th February, 1641-2, was succeeded by his son Piers Legh, of Bruche, esquire, whose portrait (copied from the original at Lyme Hall) is to be seen in the Warrington Museum. He was twice married. By his first wife he had a son of his own name, who also represented Newton in parliament, but dying without issue was succeeded in his estates by his half-sister, Frances Legh, who was born 9th June, 1670. About March, 1687, Frances was married to her relative, Peter Legh, son of Richard Legh of Lyme, esquire. A monument to her still exists in Warrington church, and upon it are enumerated her various charitable bequests, amounting to £382.

Nos. 17, 26, 29, 31, and 60. All of these shields refer to the Masceys, or Masseys, of Rixton, the members of that family having frequently used the Rixton coat alone, and having almost invariably borne the Rixton coat in the first quarters of their quartered shields. Alan de Rixton held Rixton in the reign of King John, and after him it was held successively by his descendants, all, for four generations, being named Alan. The last Alan de Rixton, who was born in the year 1355, married his only daughter and heiress, Margaret or Catherine, to Hamo, second son of Robert Masey of Tatton; who, in her right, became possessed of the Rixton estates. Seventeen members of the Masey family were successively lords of Rixton, and it was not until the year 1748 that the race became extinct. As stated above, the Rixton coat was generally borne in the first instead of the second quarter; the third quarter, which is supposed to belong to the Penington family, has not yet been accounted for, and was probably borne in error, as it was omitted in the later seals of the Masceys. The fourth quarter, which is that of Horton, came in by the marriage of Hamo or Hamnet Masey to Ellen, daughter and co-heir of William Horton of Horton, esquire, about the time of King Henry IV. The chapel, called in the *MSS.* "le Nova Capella," and "the Chappell on the South side (over) against Butler's Chappell," is the one now called the Patten Chapel. In it many of the Masceys were buried, among others Thomas Masey, Rector of Warrington from 1447 to 1464, who was brother to Hamo Masey the husband of the Horton heiress. A monumental slab in red sandstone, supposed to be his, was found during the restoration of the church, and is now placed on the South side of the churchyard. It has upon the top a floriated cross, and is ornamented round the edges with roses and quatrefoils. The door of a pew in the church, before its restoration, had upon it a quaint carving of the quartered arms (1. Rixton; 2. Massy; 3. Pennington; 4. Horton) with the inscription

RICHARD     AN° DVI.
MASSYE     1617:

The last member of the family, Francis Massy, Esquire,* who was born in the year 1703,

* His armorial seal displays the quartered arms, 1 and 4, Massy; 2, Rixton; 3, Horton; with a covered cup, Argent, for the crest. The crest was allowed by Sir William Dugdale in 1664.

# Arms formerly in Warrington Church.

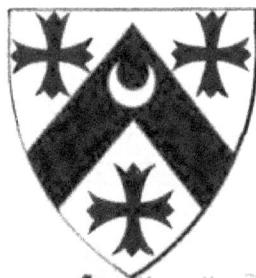

Penketh, of Penketh.　Sankey, of Sankey.　Southworth, of Southworth,

Hawarden, of Woolston, 4 quarterings.　Sankey, of Sankey, 4 quarterings.

Byron.　Haydock.　Bruche.　Plumpton.

died a bachelor 28 September 1748, bequeathing almost all his property to his kinsman George Meynell, Esq. His monument, which remained until very recently in the Massy chapel, is now placed in the crypt. The following is an exact copy of the inscription upon it :

Here lie the remains of FRANCIS MASSY Esq.
Lord of the Manors of RIXTON and GLASSBROOK in this Parish,
the last of that very antient Family :
His benevolence to mankind in general,
and his beneficence to particulars
(whom he well distinguished)
have made his name dear to his acquaintance,
among whom he had many Friends.
He was observant of the duties of his Religion :
He discharg'd with honour debts he was not oblig'd to pay,
He was very grateful to his Mother's relations,
and by his will shew'd himself just to his heirs at law,
who have erected this Monument to his memory.
These virtues make his character amiable in this world
and cannot fail of an eternal reward in the Next.
He died a Batchelor Sept'r the 27th 1748
and in the 45th year of his age.
Requiescat in pace.
D' Sephton, fecit, Manchester.

Above the inscription was a coloured shield of the quartered arms with the motto

### "NOCUMENTA DOCUMENTA."

Nos. 18, 46 and 53, are all probably notes of the same pane of glass, the escallop shells having most likely been mistaken for torteaux, as they might easily be on account of the dazzling effect of the contrasted colours of the shield. The arms are those of the family of Plumpton of Yorkshire, and were doubtless put into the church window, about the year 1365, to commemorate the marriage of Sir John le Boteler to Alicia, widow of Richard Sherburne, and daughter of Sir William Plumpton. It was customary, near to the *impaled* shield, to place shields of the arms *alone*, and in this case, as in others noted in the *MSS.*, the impaled shield has disappeared, whilst the separate single shields remain.

No. 22. This shield, which had been removed before Randle Holme took his notes, may be intended for the coat of the Urswick family ; if so, each lozenge should have been charged with a saltier Gules. Argent, on a bend Sable three lozenges of the field, was borne by the family of Carrington, but more frequently with the colours reversed. The arms are most probably those of Urswick, of which family there were two with whom the Botelers had some connexions— Sir Walter, a fellow soldier of Sir John Boteler, under the standard of John of Gaunt, and Sir Christopher Urswick, the faithful and unambitious chaplain of Henry VII., who appears in the play of *Richard III.*— and may have been known to Sir Thomas Boteler.

Nos. 27 and 30, both belonging to the family of Sankey of Sankey, and were destroyed before 1640. Moule, in his *Heraldry of Fish*, p. 193, says: "Argent on a bend Sable, three fish of the field, are the arms of the family of Sankey of Cawdwells, a manor in the parish Edlesborough, in Buckinghamshire. Sable three fish in bend between two cottises Argent, are the arms of the family of Sankey of Worcestershire. The particular species of fish is not described, but it is possible flounders are intended, from the known preference of the flat-fish to the sandy bottom of the water, and the slight play upon the name afforded by that circumstance." Mr. Moule apparently was not aware that sparlings, a fish formerly abundant at Sankey, would probably be selected by the Sankeys, of Sankey, as a suitable bearing.

We have comparatively little information about the Sankeys of Sankey, and the identification of their quarterings must, therefore, be conjectural. The three fusils in pale may be the coat of Danyers, Daniel, or Savage. The three chevronels with the birds may be a Singleton coat.

Vert a camel Or, sometimes Argent, was borne by the Cheshire family of Aldford, and by their descendants, the Fallowes, of Fallowes and Haywood, co. Chester. Although these colours differ from the glass, it is possible that the Fallowes coat was intended. Sable a camel Argent was borne by a family named Camel.

The Sankey family were settled at Sankey at a very early date, and doubtless gave name to many other Sankeys in different parts of the country, all perhaps descended from Gerald de Sanki, the carpenter, who received a whole carucate of land in Sankey by the gift of Paganus de Vilars, about the time of King Henry I. John de Sankey, one of the fifty Lancashire archers retained by Sir James Harrington, was slain at the battle of Agincourt, 1415. Thomas Sankey of Warrington, another of them, fell at Flodden Field, 1513. Edward Sankey, a parliamentarian officer, at a later period, is also supposed to have been of the same family.

Nos. 28 and 33. This is the coat of Clyderhow or Clitherowe, but its appearance "upon Boteler's wife and Boteler himself" is unaccountable. There was not any intermarriage between the Clitherowes and the Warrington Botelers, unless the first wife of Sir John Boteler, whom he married in 1356, and to whom no name is given in the pedigree, was a Clitheroe. The other coat upon the tomb is the ancient shield of Standish, the three standing dishes having been assumed at a later period.

In 1332, John, son of William de Standish, seals with a saltire between four crosses patonce, the seal being inscribed S. JOHANNIS DE STANDISSH. (*Local Gleanings*, vol. ii, p. 42, art. 532). In 1533, when the visitation of Lancashire was made, the arms borne were: Quarterly. 1st and 4th Sable, three standing dishes Argent ; 2nd and third Argent, a saltier within a bordure engrailed sable.

The monument referred to was erected to the memory of Sir William Boteler, who was born about the year 1373, died at Harfleur, before the army advanced to Agincourt, September 1415, and was buried in the Friary at Warrington. He married, on the 4th April 1404, Elizabeth, daughter of Sir Robert Standish of Standish; who, after Sir William's death, remarried to William de Ferrars of Groby, and died in the year 1440. (*Lords of Warrington*, p. 246, Cheth. Soc.)

John Donne, rector of Warrington in 1366, on his seal appended to a deed of that date exhibits a saltier engrailed, and is inscribed sigillum iohannis bonne clerici. He was admitted and instituted to the rectory of Warrington January 13th, 1361, and was afterwards chaplain to Edward the Black Prince, whom he joined in Aquitaine in the year 1370, but these arms, resembling those of Clitherowe, cannot be identified with either family.

We now come to the arms which were set up between 1572 and 1640, or which had passed unnoticed by Erdeswicke.

No. 42. The quartered coat of Hawarden of Woolston. 1st, Hawarden. 2nd, Leigh of High Leigh, ancient. 3rd, Lymme, of Lymm.* 4th, Woolston and Eaton, quarterly. The Leigh and Lymme quarters came in by the marriage of John Hawarden, of Hawarden, co. Flint, to Amery, daughter and heiress of John Leigh, of High Leigh. Their son, John Hawarden, married Annabel, daughter and heiress of Hugh Woolston, of Woolston, who brought in the Woolston and Eaton quarters. The arms in the window were most probably put up by the great-great-grandson of John and Annabel, Adam Hawarden of Woolston, esquire, who was living at the Visitation of 1567. Elizabeth, daughter and heiress of the same Adam, was married in 1574 to Alexander Standish, of Standish, esquire, and carried the Woolston estates into that family.

No. 57. Troutbeck and Boteler quarterly. It is difficult to understand why these two coats should be quartered, as we have no evidence of an heiress of the Troutbecks marrying a Boteler, nor of a Boteler heiress marrying a Troutbeck. If the arms were *impaled* instead of quartered, they would clearly have reference to Sir William Boteler and Jane, his wife, the daughter of Sir William Troutbeck. The tomb referred to, however, seems to be that of Sir William Boteler's father, Sir John Boteler, who married three wives: firstly, Margaret, daughter of Sir Peter Gerard; secondly, Elizabeth, daughter of Thomas, Lord Dacre, from whom he was divorced in 1458; and thirdly, Margaret, daughter of Thomas, Lord Stanley, the widow of Sir William Troutbeck. This monument still exists in Warrington Church.

No. 59. Ratcliff impaling Byron, or impaled with Byron, seems to have no connection with the Boteler family.

No. 60. Mascy of Rixton. Probably refers to Hamo Mascy, who married Elizabeth Boteler.

It will be seen from the above notes that the greater part of the shields were intended to commemorate the Botelers of Bewsey, the ancient lords of Warrington, and families allied with them; and it would no doubt have rendered this account more interesting had further details of their history been given. Such further information as has been obtained may be seen in the *Annals of the Lords of Warrington*, &c., 1872-3, volumes 86 and 87 of the publications of the Chetham Society.

* Borne also by Leigh of High Leigh.

# Arms from the Warrington Priory.

**Holland.**

**Lancaster.**

**Boteler.**

**de Montfort.**

**Banastre.**    **Penketh?**    **Delves.**    **Bruche.**    **Banastre.**

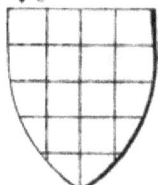    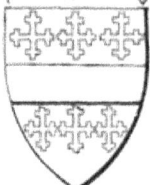

**Warren.**   **Legh, of East Hall. Gerard. Legh, of West Hall. Beauchamp.**

 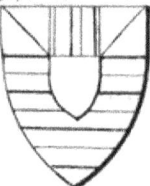   

**de Clare.**    **Mortimer.**    **de Burgh.**    **Dutton.**    **Radcliffe.**

**Standish.**    **Fitton.**    **Penketh.**    **St. George.** PH.

# PART II.

## An attempt to identify the Arms which existed in the Warrington Priory Church in the time of Queen Elizabeth.

IN No. 139 of the *Harleian Manuscripts* is a book of collections relating to local history, genealogy, &c., to which Sir Simonds D'Ewes prefixed the title following :—"An Excellent Booke, concerning most of the Lands, Descents, Coat Armours, and other passages both Legal & Historical, of the County of Chester. Collected, out of Records, Private Evidences, Epitaphs, and divers other Monuments, by LAURENCE BOSTOCKE, or, as he calls himself, *Laurence of Bostoke*."

Writing of this collection Mr. Foote Gower[*] says :—"Coeval then with the preceding, [William Smith, Rouge Dragon Pursuivant of Arms, and William Webb, M.A., who made the collections about 1590–1600, which were published by Daniel King[†]] was LAURENCE BOSTOKE ; or, as he usually stiled himself, from the place of his birth, and habitation—de Bostoke. The materials he has left behind him are extremely valuable and are contained in one Folio Volume, closely written, in a very bad hand. The Articles are Miscellaneous ; *Descents, Pedigrees, Notes of Families, Extracts from Old Deeds and Records ;* and, what is above all, *an accurate visitation of most of our Churches before that sacrilegious Destruction in the Civil War.* Whatever was remarkable here, he has attempted to delineate. But he was a bad draughtsman ; and though his designs may be faithful representations, yet they are by no means the Work of any Artist. Contemporary with *Laurence de Bostoke* was SAMPSON ERDESWICKE, &c."

From the late Dr. Ormerod's *History of Cheshire* we learn that Bostoke was the great-grandson of an illegitimate brother of the last heir-male of the Bostock family, William Bostock, who died about the year 1482 ; and that he was, in addition to his genealogical and other manuscripts, "the author of an historical poem, of considerable merit, on the subject of the Saxon and Norman Earls of Chester."

---

[*] A Sketch of the Materials for a new History of Cheshire : &c., &c., in a letter to Thomas Falconer, Esq., of the City of Chester. Sold by Mr. Lawton, bookseller in Chester, and Mr. Bathurst, bookseller in Fleet Street, London, 1771.

[†] Published in 1656, and usually known by the name of King's Vale Royal of England, though King used a very defective copy, amd apparently garbled the text.

We have, however, seen that his collections were made at the end of the sixteenth century, about the same time as Erdeswicke's *Notes of Warrington Church*, to which they therefore form a fitting companion here.

In the *Harleian Manuscripts*, No. 2129, is a copy of the notes taken by Bostoke, made about 1640, having rude drawings of some of the figures made from his descriptions. Some of these figures have been engraved in Pennant's *Tour*, Baines' *Lancashire, History of Warrington Friary,** &c.; and, in the *History of Lancashire* are, by mistake, stated to have been in the parish church.

Of this second *MS.*, as well as of Bostoke's, which is frequently referred to in the above and other historical works, it has been thought advisable to give a copy. In describing both sets of notes, the same plan is followed as in the Warrington Church notes by Erdeswick and Holme, with the exception of the asterisks, which are unnecessary.

## EXTENDED BLAZON OF LAURENCE BOSTOKE'S NOTES OF THE ARMS, &c., IN THE AUSTIN FRIARY, AT WARRINGTON.

### (*Harleian MS.* 139.)

At Warrington in the Chancell w<sup>th</sup>in the Priory their [there] in the glasse wyndowes are these monewments; on on[e] wyndow ar[e] these armes in ye m'gent [margin] in the highest of y<sup>e</sup> same windowe :

[1.] A drawing of three birds upon a shield.

[2.] An outline shield with this description written within it : Ar[gent], three fowles lyke howlets w'out [without] legges Azure [Possibly *Penketh of Penketh*], and the same coat of arms with a label of three points Argent.

[3.] In the same wyndowe in the mydle of the same ys y<sup>e</sup> p'erlsonage of a man armed all in male [mail] from topp to to[e] w<sup>t</sup> a blewe robe girded about hym, a naked sweard in his ryght hand, and in his left hand holding a lance w<sup>th</sup> a banner of th' armes of *Holland*, that ys Azure a lyon r[ampant], Argent gardant w<sup>t</sup> flewer de luces symme [semée] Ar[gent].

[4.] On his right hand in lyke man[ner] a man holding in his right hand a shild of armes as in the m'gent [margin] w<sup>th</sup> his hand on his sweard. In the margin is a shield Sable, a cross patonce Or.

* *History of Warrington Friary*, printed for the Chetham Society, 1872, pp. 80, and 4 *plates*. *Chetham Miscellanies*, vol. iv. To this work the reader is referred for further information about the Friary

[5.] On his ryght hand in lyke man[ner] a man armed holding in his ryght hand a lance w^t a banner of armes, on y^e w^ch as in y^t m'gent [Gules, three lions passant guardant in pale Or ; a label of three points Argent] w^t his hand uppon his sweard, their three garments blewe ; girdles and scabbards gold. [To the drawing of the banner in the margin he adds this note :—] three lions pas. gardant Or, drowen awt Ar[gent] w^t a penne [which probably means that the lights on the golden lions were scratched out so as to show the plain glass and give a better effect].

In the second wyndowe on the northe syd (side), in the height of the wyndowe as in the m'gent.

[6.] Bendy, Or and Azure. [*de Montfort.*]

[7.] Or, three chevronels Gules. [*de Clare.*]

[8.] Or, a cross Gules. [*de Burgh.*]

[9.] In the mydle of the wyndowe the p[er]sonage of a man armed at all points in male, w^t a robe colored Or, gyrded w^t a sweard on his side Vert, holding in his hand a shyld w^ch armes as in the m'gente [Argent, a cross patonce Sable].

[10.] Drawing of a shield, checky Or and Gules, above which is the word *Butler*. [This is certainly not a *Butler* coat.]

Over the hyghe Alter these armes fyrst :

[11.] *Holland* [as No. 3] the[n].

[12.] *Butler, barron de Warrington* [Azure, a bend between six covered cups Or] then a shild.

[13.] Or, a lion ra[mpant] Gewles [*Legh*]. then

[14.] Ar[gent], a lyon r[ampant] Gewles [*Legh*]. then

[15.] Azure, a lion ram[pant] Argent [? ermine, crowned Or. *Gerard*].

On the fourthe syde of the same chauncell these armes in the m'gent in the toppe of the wyndowe :

[16.] Drawing of a shield, Gules, a cross Or [? *de Burgh*].

[17.] Drawing of a shield, Barry of four, Or and Azure, an inescocheon Argent ; on a chief of the second three pallets between two gyrons of the first. *Mortymar.*

[17a.] In the mydle of y^e same wyndowe beneth a man armed in male, w^t a robe Or, holding a naked sweard in his ryght hand, and in his left hand a lance w^t a banner of th' armes of Holland as in y^e m'gent. In the margin, the banner is divided per fesse, on the upper part is written " Azure," and on the lower " Holland."

[18.] On his left hand a man lykewyse armed in male from tope to to:, w^t a robe Or, girdle and swear[d] Vert, holding a shild of armes Argent, a cross patonce Sable [? *Banastre*] in his right hand, his left hand on his sweard.

[19.] In the body of the Churche, on the south syde, in a wyndow ys th'
armes of *Butler* [as No. 12] in on[e] shyld, and

[20.] *Delves* [Argent, a chevron Gules, fretty Or, between three delves or
turves Sable] in another shild.

[21.] In an other wyndowe on the same syde, ys a shyld of *Delves* w' a
crownet gold, and the same joyned hard to the shyld [*i.e.*, a coronet reaching the
width of the top of the shield, and touching it the whole way across].

[22.] Upon the steple [*i.e.*, tower] w'hin the Churche carved or graven in stone
ys *Butlers* single coat,

[23.] th' armes of [the Isle of] Man [Gules, three legs conjoined at the thighs,
flexed in triangle Argent, garnished and spurred Or].

[24.] *Delves* [as before],

[25.] the shyld w' three byrds in yt [as Nos. 1 and 2] as in the glasse
wyndowe afforesaid,

[26.] a shyld of the Ægle foot [? *Torbock* Or, an eagle's leg couped at the
thigh Gules, on a chief indented Azure, three plates] and these

[27.] A drawing of a shield [Argent] a chevron between three pierced mullets
Sable [? *Bruche of Bruche*]; besydes armes uppon shilds in the rofe of the
Chansell that I cannot discerne, saving

[28.] *Beauchamp* [Gules, a fesse between six cross crosslets Or].

[29.] *Butler* [as before].

[30.] *Dutton* [Quarterly. Argent and Gules, in the 2nd and 3rd a fret Or].

[31.] *Radcliffe* [? Argent, a bend engrailed Sable].

[32.] *Holland* [as before].

[33.] *Fytton* [Argent, on a bend Azure, three garbs Or], and the rest
amonteth to 41 shylds, etc.

I suppose the said three byrds [No. 25] to be Kynge fyshars, because of
yeer [their] long beaks.

[34.] There is y' pycture of a man carved in wood, crosse legged, armed in
male from head to fote, w'h a shyld uppon his left arme, and both his hands uppon
his swearde, as he wold put yt owt, but th' armes of his shyld ys worne away ;
also in y' said chancell ys a monument in allabaster w' this sup[er]scription.

HIC JACET LANCEL[OTI] VICECOMITATIBUS . . . . . . DNS. WAITTS BOTTLER,
BARON DE WARYNGTON Q[UI] OBIIT APUD HARFFLER IN VIGILIA SCI. MATHEI
APOSTOLI A°. DNI. 1415. ET DNA . . . . . . QUE QUIDE[M] ERAT UXOR, AC ÆIA UXOR'
JOHIS DNIS DE WARBLETON OF WARINGTON. ETC.

[36.] These arms on her brest on the pyctures of a man and woman  Drawing
of a shield . . . . . on a saltier . . . . . . a mullet . . . . . . [This refers to the above
monument].

[*Harleian MS.* 2129.]

[*Copied from the Bostoke MS., with additions, &c.*]

At Warrington in the Chancesell w'in the Priory there in the glasse windows are these monyments, on on[e] windowe are these Armes in every gent [*in y' m'gent* in the original by Bostoke] in the highest of the same window :

[37.] [Drawing of a shield Argent, three owls Azure] three fowles lik[e] owles. *Falcons, this is the arms of Atherton, John Prestwich.\** [No. 1.]

[38.] An outline shield with the note "the same agayne *Penketh*," and another shield of the three owls with a label of three points untinctured, marked "id[e]m." [No. 2.] Then follow drawings of three knights described by Bostoke, Nos. 3, 4 and 5, very probably drawn from his description only.

[39.] [The first figure is the one holding a shield Sable, charged with a cross patonce Or.— No. 4.]

[40.] [The middle figure is that with the arms of Holland upon his banner.—No. 3.]

[41.] [The figure to the right is the one described under No. 5].

In the second wyndowe one the North side in the high of the wyndow these Armes.

[42.] Drawing as No. 6 ; Bendy, Or and Azure. *Mountford.*

[43.] Drawing as No. 7 ; Or, three chevronels Gules. *Clare.*

[44.] Drawing as No. 8 ; Or, a cross Gules. *Burgh.*

[45.] In the midle of the wyndowe this pictur [which answers exactly to the description given under No. 9, the robe being Or, and the sword sheath Vert, but the shield which the knight holds in his hand has upon it a cross patonce *untinctured* ].

Over the high Alter these Armes folowing

---

\* This note was apparently added by "Sir" John Prestwich, "Bart.," the author of a rather scarce book, printed in 1787, called "*Prestwich's Respublica*; or a Display of the Honors, Ceremonies and Ensigns of the Common Wealth, Under the Protectorship of Oliver Cromwell, together with The Names, Armorial Bearings, Flags and Pennons, of the Different Commanders of the English, Scotch, Irish, Americans and French. (Arms of Prestwich and quartering, impaling Hall.) And An Alphabetical Roll of the Names and Armorial Bearings of Upwards of Three Hundred Families of the Present Nobility and Gentry of England, Scotland, Ireland, &c., &c. London: Printed by and for J. Nichols MDCCLXXXVII." 4to, pp. 279. This work does not seem to have been completed ; it is very curious and shows that "Sir John" was a most eccentric man. It is more than doubtful whether he had any claim to the title of baronet.

The birds in the arms of Atherton are *not* owls but falcons, as Prestwich notes ; but the colours were very different from those of the arms in the Priory window, being Gules, three falcons, close, Or.

D

[46.] A blank shield, *Holland* [as No. 11], then

[47.] A blank shield, *Butler Barron de Warrington* [No. 12].

[48.] *Powis* [possibly a lion rampant, a charge frequently given to the name of Powis] then this

[49.] Drawing of a shield, Or, a lion rampant Gules, *Leigh of Westhall* [No. 13], and this

[50.] Drawing of a shield, Argent, a lion rampant Gules, *Legh of Esthall* [No. 14], and this last

[51.] Drawing of a shield Azure, a lion rampant Argent [No. 15], *Montalt*. One the south ["fourthe" in original by Bostoke] syd[e] of the sam[e] Chancel thes[e] Armes folowing one the topp of the wyndow.

[52.] Drawing of a shield Gules, a cross Or, as No. 16. [Probably *de Burgh* with the colours reversed.]

[53.] Drawing of a shield, checky Or and Gules as No. 10. *Waren*. [If this be Warren, it should be Or and Azure.]

[54.] Drawing of the Mortimer shield as No. 17. *Mortymer*.

[55.] In the mydle of the same last wyndow beneath a man armed in male w[t] a robe Or, holding a naked sword in his right hand, and [in] his left hand a Lance with a banner of the arms of *Holland*. [As Nos. 3 and 17a.]

[56.] On his left hand a man likewise in male from topp to the too [toe] w[t] a rob[e] Or, girded w[t] sword V[ert], houlding this shild of armes a cross patonce [untinctured] in his right hand, his left hand one his sword as one the other syde of this leaf more playnner appeareth. [This refers to the drawing No. 39, being the same as No. 4 in Bostoke's *MS.*]

[57 and 58.] In the body of the church on the south side in a wyndowe ys th' arms of *Butler* in one shild, and *Delves* in another shild. [This describes Nos. 19 and 20.]

[59.] In another wyndow on the same syde ys a shild of the Armes of *Delves* w[t] a coronet Or, over the same joyned hard to the shild. [This describes No. 21.]

[60.] Upon the steple w'in the church carved or graven in stone ys *Butler's* single coat [No. 22].

[61.] the Armes of *Man* [No. 23].

[62.] the shild w[t] three byrds in yt as in the glasse windowe aforesayd [No. 25].

[63.] a shild of the egle foot [No. 26].

[64.] and thes[e] . . . . . . a chevron between three mullets . . . . . [No. 27], besyde Armes uppon shilds in the roufe of the chansell that I cannot discerne saving

[65.] *Beauchamp* [No. 28].

[66.] *Butler* [No. 29].

[67.] *Radclyf* [No. 31].

[68.] *Holland* [No. 32].

[69.] *Fitton* [No. 33], and the rest amonteth to forty-one shilds etc.   I suppose the sayd three birds to be king fishers because of their long beaks.

[70.] There is the picture of a man carved in wode the armes of his shild is woren away.   [No. 34.]

[71.] Also in the sayd chancesell is a monyment in Allabaster w⁺ this sup[er]scription : HIC JACET LANCELOTI VICOMITATIS DNS. WAITTS BOTETER. BARON DE WARYNGTO[N] Q[UI] OBIIT APUD HAREFLU[R] IN VIGILIA SCI. MATHEI APOSTOLI. AN⁰. DM. 1415. DNA. QUE QUIDE[M] ERAT UXOR AC AIA. UXOR JOHIS DNIS. DE WARHLETON or WARINGTON, &c.   [No. 35.]

These arms on her brest on a saltire, a mullet, [as No. 36, being the ancient coat of *Standish*].

# Notes.

The birds in Nos. 1, 2, 37, and 38, although Bostoke says that they are like owls, would seem more probably to be popinjays, and the bearing to be that of the *Penkeths of Penketh*, near Warrington, whose arms were Argent, three popinjays Azure, sometimes with a chevron between them. Two of the shields display the plain coat, and the third has a label, the distinctive mark of the eldest son during his father's lifetime. Dodsworth saw the same arms in Farnworth Church in his time, and describes the coat as Argent, three king fishers Azure, feet Sable. The Penkeths would probably be commemorated in the Priory windows on account of some benefaction, and also because one of the family, Thomas Penketh, born about the year 1437, was afterwards Provincial of the Hermit Friars of St. Augustine in England and Ireland. (*Warrington Friary*, p. 44.)

No. 23 probably commemorates the marriage of Sir John Boteler with Margaret Stanley in 1459.

Nos. 3, 11, 17a, 32, 46, 55, and 68 are the arms of the very influential family of *Holland*. The knight is most probably Sir Robert de Holland. One of the family, John de Holand, was a Warrington Friar, and was ordained deacon in 1371. (*Warrington Friary*, p. 11.)

Nos. 4, 9, 18, 39, 45, and 56. On these shields the colours are sometimes reversed ; they are, most probably, intended to commemorate some members of the family of *Banastre*.*

Nos. 5 and 41. This figure has been generally supposed to represent *Thomas*, Earl of Lancaster, Leicester, Derby and Lincoln, and Steward of England, the eldest son and heir of Edmond Crouchback. He sided with the barons in his hatred of Piers Gaveston, for whose death he had a pardon, 16 October, 7 Edward II, 1313. He afterwards took up arms to expel Hugh le Despencer, the younger, and with the other barons was the means of his death. The barons being afterwards defeated, Earl Thomas was taken prisoner at Borough-bridge and beheaded at his castle of Pontefract.

It is probable that Thomas, Earl of Lancaster, would be commemorated in the Priory windows with his supporters, Sir Robert de Holland and Sir Adam Banastre. The glazier has, however, put upon the banner of the first named person the arms of the Prince of Wales, Gules, three lions passant guardant in pale Or, a label Argent.

Sir Robert Holland was the father of Thomas Holland, Earl of Kent, K.G. Writing of this family, the late Mr. Beltz, *Lancaster Herald*,† says : The members of this prosperous family, of whom, in the course of three generations, there were seven knights of the garter,

---

* For accounts of the Banastre family, barons of Newton in Makerfield, see "'The Fee of Makerfield,'" *Hist. Soc. Lanc. and Chesh.*, new series, vol. xii, p. 81; "The Arms of Banastre and Langton," by William Langton, Esq., *Herald and Genealogist*, vol. vii, p. 440; and *The Visitation of Lancashire* in 1533, edited by William Langton, Esq., Chetham Soc., vol. xcviii. Sir Adam Banastre, at the Stepney tournament in 2 Edward II, bore Argent, a cross flory Sable, but it is not known that these arms were ever borne by the barons of Newton.

† *Memorials of the Most Noble Order of the Garter, &c.*, by George Frederick Beltz, K.H., Lancaster Herald. London. Pickering, 1841. But the author was under a mistake about the Hollands being an inconsiderable family. They were an ancient knightly family of large possessions (*Hist. Lanc.*, vol. iii, p. 351 *et passim*).

derived no particular lustre from ancestry. Sir Robert Holland, the father of the Earl of Kent, was the first of a gentle but inconsiderable stock settled at Holland, in Lancashire, who acquired any celebrity. He had served in the wars of Edward I in Scotland, but owed his rise and advancement to his situation of secretary to the mighty and unfortunate Thomas Plantagenet, Earl of Lancaster, through whose power and influence he obtained divers valuable grants in Derbyshire, as well as the government of Beeston Castle, in Cheshire, from Edward II. He was further enriched by his marriage with Maud, one of the daughters and co-heirs of Alan, lord La Zouche of Ashby; and, soon after that event, summoned to parliament amongst the barons of the realm. Having attained this eminence, he ill requited the generosity which had conducted him to it; and deserted, if not betrayed, his illustrious patron in the hour of peril. Certain adherents of the fallen and popular prince seized the unfaithful servant in a wood near Henley, in Oxfordshire, and struck off his head.

The founder of the ancient family of Banastre was Robert Banastre, who came to England with William the Conqueror, and obtained the manor of Prestatyn in Wales. Of the same family was Sir Thomas Banastre, K.G., whose garter-plate displays Argent, a cross cercelée (or patonce) Sable, with the crest of a peacock sejant proper. Sir Adam Banastre, whose figure we suppose to be represented in the stained glass in the Priory, was Lord of Shevington in 1287, and in 1310 possessed lands in Lower Darwen and Aghton in Black-burnshire, and at the asserted instigation of Edward II, raised a tumult against his liege lord, the Earl of Lancaster, and was ultimately beheaded in 1316.* His wife, Margaret (who held lands in Shevington, Aghton, and Lower Darwen in 1324), was daughter of Sir Robert de Holland.

Another member of the family, Henry Banastre, was compromised by his adherence to Thomas, Earl of Lancaster, and obtained a pardon for all felonies and trespasses committed by him up to August last past, tested at York, 1st November, 12 Edward II. (*Parliamentary Writs*, vol. ii, pt. ii, p. 130.) This *may* be the man whose effigy was recorded along with the Earl and Holland.†

Geoffrey Banastre, another member of the family, was Prior of Warrington in 1404, and on June 3, 1419, was presented by the Abbot of Whalley to the vicarage of Blackburn, where, in 1453, he founded a chantry, and died about October 1457.‡

The arms of Thomas, Earl of Lancaster, were Gules, three lions passant guardant in pale Or, with a label Azure, upon each point of which there were three golden fleurs-de-lys. His large armorial seal, which is engraved in Sandford's *Genealogical History of the Kings of England*, p. 102, has, upon the obverse, the figure of the Earl on horseback, his shield, surcoat, and the caparisons of his horse in two places, displaying these arms, the label having three points; on the reverse is a large shield of the arms occupying the greater part of the surface of the seal, and here, with the same arms, the label has five points, each being charged with three fleurs-de-lys. The seal is as large as that of the king, and has the following legend both on the obverse and **reverse**: SIGILLVM THOME: COMITIS: LANCASTRIE: ET: LEYCESTRIE: SENESCALLI ANGLIE.

The arms of the Prince of Wales, *as eldest son* of the king, were the royal arms

* Beltz. Order of the Garter.    † Mr. Langton's notes.    ‡ *Warrington Friary.*

differenced by a white label, and were so borne by all three Edwards during the lifetime of their fathers, Edward the third's label having sometimes three and sometimes five points.

The arms of "Lancaster" came to have the white label upon the title being vested in the king, Henry IV being both King and Duke of Lancaster, but his father, John of Gaunt, did not use the white label, each point of his being charged with three ermine spots.

Nos. 6 and 42. The arms of Simon de Montfort, Earl of Leicester, a powerful friend of the Austin Friars, who was canonized after his death.

The arms of the Warrington Friary seem to have been founded upon the de Montford coat, for they were either Bendy [Or] and [Azure], a chief [Gules], or [?Or], two bends [?Azure], a chief [?Gules], and are displayed, with the arms of Boteler of Bewsey, upon the Friary seal attached to a deed dated 24 June 1422.

Simon de Montfort, with other powerful barons, rose in arms against Henry III, attempting to compel the removal of many grievances; he was, however, defeated and slain by Prince Edward at the battle of Evesham, 4 August, 1265.

The following passage from the *Brute Chronicle* in reference to the Earl of Leicester and the miracles performed in his name after his death, is both quaint and curious:

"Wanne king Herry hadde the victori at Evesham, and Simonde the erle was y-sley by the helpe of Gilberte off Clare, erle of Gloucestre, the wiche was in the warde of the foreseid Simon by the assignemente of kynge Herry. And afterward the same Gilberte was with king Herry in the forseide bateille of Evesham, were-thurgh [through which] the for-seide Simon was destroiedde; and thatt was grete harme to the comens of Englonde, thatt so gode man was destroiedde, ffor he was dede for the comenne profite of the same ffolke, and therefore God hathe schewed ffor him many grete miracules to diverse ffolkes of her [their] maladies and grevawnee, werefore thei have be[en] heledde."

Another interesting account of these miracles will be found in *Rishanger's Chronicle*, pub-lished by the Camden Society, 1840; in this book there are notices of the Montfort miracles at Weruntone-super-Merse (Warrington), which have been translated by Dr. Kendrick as follows:

"MARGERY DE LABURD, of Weryntone, having spasms, and dysentery, and swimming in the head, for five weeks, from pain of which she lost her reason, applied the Earl's fillet, and having wrapped a penny in it, she got better. Of this the whole town of Werintone beareth testimony.

"ALYNE DE FAMELESBURYE (*sic*), having a certain obscure infirmity for five weeks, applied the Earl's fillet, and recovered. Of which the aforesaid town bears witness.

"WYON DE WERINTONE suffered from a blast in his right leg for two years. He dreamed that he was in a certain place where the Earl was, and it seemed to him that the Earl breathed upon him, and his whole complaint vanished.

"GYLBERT DE WERINTONE, having a very painful blast for four years, applied the Earl's fillet, and got well. Of this the whole town of Werintone beareth testimony.

"JAMES DE WERINTONE had a blast, which is called *fetre*, for ix weeks; applying the Earl's fillet, and wrapping up a penny, he got well. These six (*sic*) happened in the afore-said town upon the Merse, that is upon the banks of that river.

"ALICIA, SISTER OF WILLIAM, *the rector of the church at Werintone*, suffering from a sudden windy swelling on the right side of the head, and right side of the face down to the neck, in consequence of which it was feared that she would be carried off by a sudden death. and she listening to the counsel of certain of her attendants, applied Earl Simon's fillet, and recovered. Of this fact the aforesaid William beareth witness, who brought the votive candle to Evesham.

"*Memorandum*, that the said William told me a wonderful thing, saying — that when he, after the battle fought at Evesham, took with him into the country some earth from the spot where the Earl fell, and had taken it into his keeping in a piece of cloth, a certain layman of the name of (*sic*) was sick even to death, so that he had received the holy Eucharist, and lay for two days without speech. Earl Simon appearing to him in his sleep, as it seemed to him, told him that he should beseech the said William, that he would give him a small portion of the said earth, which he had in his keeping, and that he should mix it with water, and use it for drink ; which being done, the said patient recovered his health.

"SIR HELISEUS, *dean of Weryntou*, deprived of sight for three years, recovered : having applied the fillet of the Earl. Of this, witness is borne by all who speak of it between Kibbel and Merse, that is, between those two rivers.

"ROGER, *dean of Werintone*, confined with so severe an infirmity in the right knee, on the Sunday before Christmas of the present year, that he could not move from the place where he sat, nor bear that any one should lend an helping hand, nor an unguent, nor a plaster, at last called to mind the martyrdom of Earl Simon, and was well immediately ; so that on Christmas day he fulfilled his sacred duties without hindrance, nor hath he hitherto felt any symptom of infirmity in any other part. Testimony of this is borne by Richard called the hermit, who brought his candle to Evesham."

Nos. 7 and 43. The arms of the family of the *de Clares*, Earls of Gloucester, &c. According to many authorities the Austin Friars were first brought to England, and settled at Clare in the diocese of Norwich, by de Clare, Earl of Gloucester, and though other authors state that the Friars came to England under various other auspices, the continual appearance of the de Clare arms in the friaries throughout the kingdom shows that the friars had some strong reason for holding that family in particular honour, so that probably the statement that the de Clares were their first founders is in the main correct.

The reason that the arms of de Clare, de Burgh and Mortimer were erected in the priories is shown in the following quaint lines given in Weever's *Funerall Monuments*, first edition, 1631, p. 737. Weever copied the verses (which are in both Latin and English, the latter being in eighteen verses) from an ancient roll in the possession of that admirable herald Augustine Vincent, *Windsor*, whose memoirs were written by Sir Harris Nicolas.

The verses are headed in red letters.

"This Dialoge betwix a seculer askyng, and a Frere answering, at the graue of Dame Johan of Acres ; sheweth the lineall descent of the Lordis of the honoure of Clare, fro the tyme of the fundation of the Freeris in the same honoure, the yere of our Lord a M.CCXLVIII. unto the first of May, the yere, a M.CCCCLX."

The pictures of the Secular Priest and the Friere (says Weever) are curiously limned upon the parchment.

       \*     \*     \*     \*     \*

" *A.* This Gilbertis fadir was that noble knight
Sir Richard of Clare : so sey all and sum
Which for Freris loue that Giles* hight,
And his boke clepid, *De Regimine principum* ;
Made furst Frere Augustines to Ingelonde cum,
Therein to duelle, and for that dede,
In heuen God graunte hym joye to mede.

*Q.* But leterally who was telle me.
This Ricardis wiff whom thou preisest so ?
*A.* The Countes of Hereford and Mauld hight she,
Whiche whan deth the knotte had undoo
Of temporal spousaile, bitwixt hem twoo,
With diuers parcels encresid our fundatioun,
Liche as our Monumentys make declaration.

*Q.* Of the furst Gilbert who was the wyff ?
*A.* Dame Mauld, a Ladye ful honourable
Borne of the Ulsters as shewith ryff
Hir aarmes of glas in the Est gable,
And for to God thei wolde ben acceptable,
Her Lord and she with an holy entent
Made up our Chirche fro the fundament.

Now to Dame Johan turne we ageyn
Latter Gilbertis wyff, as so forne seyd is
Which lyeth here.   *Q.* Was she baryn ?
*A.* Nay sir.   *Q.* Say me what fruite was this ?
*A.* A brawnshe of right grete joye I wis
*Q.* Man or woman ?   *A.* A Lady Bright ;
*Q.* What was hir name ?   *A.* Elizabeth she hight.

*Q.* Who was her husband ?   *A.* Sir John of Burgh,
Eire of the Ulstris ; so conjoyned be
Ulstris armes and Gloucestris thurgh and thurgh,
As shewith our wyndowes in housis thre,
Dortour,† chapiter hous, and Fraitour,‡ which she
Made oute the ground, both plauncher§ and wal.
*Q.* And who the rofe?‖   *A.* She alone did al.

*Q.* Had she ony Issue ?   *A.* Yea sir sikerly ¶
*Q.* What ?   *A.* a doughtur.   *Q.* what name had she ?

---

* Egidius Romanus, a pupil of Thomas Aquinas, and afterwards Bishop of Berry, who, about 1316, was author of this book.
    † Dormitory.        ‡ Refectory.        § Wood work, flooring.        ‖ Roof.        ¶ Certainly

*A.* Liche hir modir Elisabeth sothely.*
*Q.* Who euir the husbonde of hir might be?
*A.* King Edwards Son the third was he
    Sir Lionel, which buried is hir by,
    As for such a Prince too sympilly.+

*Q.* Left he onye frute this Prince mighty?
*A.* Sir yea, a doughter and Philip she hight,
    Whom Sir Edmond Mortimer wedded truly,
    First Erle of the Marche, a manly knight.
    Whos Son sir Roger by title of right,
    Lefte heire anothir Edmonde ageyn:
    Edmonde left noone but deid **bareyn**."

     \*     \*     \*     \*     \*

Nos. 8, 10, 44, 52; 10, 53; 17, 54; and 28, 65. The arms of the *de Burghs*, Earls of Ulster; the *Warrens*, Earls of Warren and Surrey; the *Mortimers*, Earls of March; and the *Beauchamps*, Earls of Warwick; all allied in blood with the de Clares, and all very important families. These arms are to be seen on various buildings, &c., in almost every county in the kingdom.

Nos. 12, 19, 22, 29, 47, 57, 60 and 66, all commemorate the Botelers of Bewsey, Barons of Warrington, who were benefactors of the Friary, the Parish Church, and the founders of the Butler Chantry and Free Grammar School, as well as of the markets. Of this family full particulars will be found in *The Annals of the Lords of Warrington*, (one of the publications of the Chetham Society.) It will, however, be well to notice that two of the monuments contained in Bostoke's notes belong to this family.

Nos. 34 and 70. The wooden monument was probably that of William, fitz Almeric, le Botiller, who was sheriff of Lancashire in 1256, and probably the founder of the priory.

Nos. 35 and 71. The alabaster monument was erected to the memory of Sir William fitz John le Botiller, Knt., Knight of the Bath, born about 1373, married to Elizabeth Standish, daughter of Sir Robert Standish of Standish, Knight (whose arms appear in a small escutcheon on the breast of Dame Elizabeth in the effigy). This Sir William set sail with Henry V. when that king went into France on the expedition during which the battle of Agincourt was fought. Sir William, however, did not fight at Agincourt, but died at Harfleur, September 20th, 1415. The inscription probably read:

HIC JACET . . . . . . DOMINUS WILLIELMUS LE BOTELER, BARO DE WARYNGTON, QUI OBIIT APUD HAREFLUR IN VIGILIA SANCTI MATHEI APOSTOLI ANNO DOMINI MCCCCXV ET DOMINA [ELIZABETHA] QUÆ QUIDEM ERAT UXOR [EJUS] AC ALICIA UXOR JOHANNIS DOMINI DE WARRINGTON.

Here lies Sir William Boteler, Baron of Warrington, who died at Harfleur in the Vigil of St. Mathew the Apostle in the year of our Lord 1415; and the lady [Elizabeth] who was his wife; and Alicia the wife of John [Boteler] Lord of Warrington.

        \* Truly.        + Simply.

E

Nos. 13, 14, 49 and 50, most probably commemorate members of the families of *Legh of East Hall* and *Leigh of West Hall* in High Leigh, co. Chester.

Nos. 15 and 51 is called, in the later copy, *Moultalt*, it may be that coat, but it is more probably the shield of the *Gerards* of Bryn, Azure, a lion rampant Ermine, crowned Or, the two arms being often mistaken one for the other.

Nos. 20, 21, 24, 58, and 59, all refer to the family of *Delves of Dodington*, co. Chester, with whom the Botelers intermarried, and some member of the family may also have been a benefactor of the Warrington Priory. See notes to the arms in the Parish Church, 21 and 41*a*.

Nos. 23 and 61 are the arms of the *Isle of Man.*

Nos. 26, 48 and 63 are, I have little doubt, the arms of *Torbock of Torbock* ; one of this family, Dame Cecilia Torboke, by her will, dated 7 March, 1466, having made a bequest to the "Blacke Frerys of Weryngton." (*Warrington in* 1465, Cheth. Soc., p. xxxvi.)

Nos. 27 and 64, most probably the coat of the local family of *Bruche of Bruche*, placed there because some of them had been benefactors of the priory.

No. 30, which is omitted in the later copy of the *MS.*, is the coat of *Dutton of Dutton*, Sir Thomas de Dutton, who died 1379, founded a perpetual chantry in the Priory Church, and another member of the family, Sir Lawrence, was also a benefactor.

Nos. 31 and 67. The arms of the *Radcliffe* family, probably placed there on account of a benefaction.

Nos. 33 and 69. The arms of the *Fyttons* of Bolyn, co. Chester, or Great Harwood, co. Lanc., which may have been placed in the priory on account of some benefaction.

Many of the coats of arms in the above *MS.* are those of families not only of local importance, but of the greatest importance in the history of England in the middle ages ; men whose names even at this remote period are as well known as those of the most prominent peers and politicians of the present day. This being the case, it is not possible to identify them with the Warrington Priory, except perhaps as munificent benefactors of the order of St. Augustine in England. The same may be said of many of the arms formerly existing in our churches and elsewhere ; for in the middle ages it was the custom to set up the armorial bearings of the king or queen in private houses, frequently accompanied by shields of arms of families of local or general importance.

John Bossewell, in his *Workes of Armorie*, published in the year 1572, after a woodcut and description of the arms of "our moste dreade soueraigne Ladie, Queen Elizabeth, that nowe is our chiefe Gouernour vnder Christe, [and] ought of al estates to be knowne, and knowne to be reuerenced, and honoured, as thereby we maie woorthily confesse, and acknowledg y͏ᵉ Soueraigntie, Royaltie, Preheminence, and Dignitie of her, and her Auncestors magnificence &c." adds, that any person "seinge the same afterwarde in any Churche, Castle, or other place," shall at once "know the same, and remember the reuerence therunto due : and not that onely, but will breake out, and say, *God saue the Queene, God saue her Grace.* Which woordes so saide, and hearde of others, bringeth all the hearers in remembrance of their obedience, and ductie to her, being our most lawful Prince, and Gouernour. And these Armes are of all men, liuing vnder her, & her Lawes, and within all her dominions, to be extolled, and set up in the highest place of our Churches, houses & mansions, aboue all other estates & degrees, who so euer they be."

This was no empty figure of speech on the part of Bossewell, for the custom to which he refers was then as prevalent among loyal subjects as that of bowing to the altar on entering a church,* and what was true of the arms of the sovereign, was true in a lesser degree of the arms of the ancient nobility; and it was a like respect for, and loyalty to, the higher powers that, in many instances, caused the shields of great personages to be placed in churches and other edifices.

It will be seen from the above notes that armorial bearings are a very useful help to history, and any one who will learn their true meaning will very frequently be enabled to ascertain the dates and builders, or owners, of castles, monuments, &c., and be assisted in the identification of many other very interesting objects of antiquity. But this is only true to a certain point; for, about the end of the fifteenth century began the absurd practice of assuming arms without authority, merely on the ground sometimes even of a remote similarity in the surname, a practice which is only too common in the present day. Such spurious and fantastic assumptions, like sham titles, will only tend to confuse and mislead future historians.

* The *Herald and Genealogist*, edited by the late John Gough Nichols, F.S.A., vol. ii, p. 94.

# INDEX.

F

CHARLES SIMMS AND CO., PRINTERS, MANCHESTER.

www.ingramcontent.com/pod-product-compliance
Lightning Source LLC
Chambersburg PA
CBHW021429090426
42739CB00009B/1419